Seeds, Bees, Butterflies, and More!

POEMS FOR
TWO VOICES

Poems by
CAROLE GERBER

Illustrated by
EUGENE YELCHIN

Henry Holt and Company   New York

Henry Holt and Company, LLC, *Publishers since 1866*
175 Fifth Avenue, New York, New York 10010
mackids.com

Henry Holt® is a registered trademark of Henry Holt and Company, LLC.

Library of Congress Cataloging-in-Publication Data
Gerber, Carole.
Seeds, bees, butterflies, and more! : poems for two voices / poems by Carole Gerber ;
illustrated by Eugene Yelchin. — 1st ed.
p.   cm.
ISBN 978-0-8050-9211-0
I. Yelchin, Eugene, ill. II. Title.
PS3557.E657S44 2013   811'.54—dc23   2012011490

First Edition—2013 / Designed by April Ward
The artist used graphite and gouache on watercolor paper
to create the illustrations for this book.

Printed in China by South China Printing Co. Ltd., Dongguan City, Guangdong Province
1   3   5   7   9   10   8   6   4   2

3788

To Linda Damato, sister of my heart
—C. G.

To Sally and April
—E. Y.

How to Read These Poems

These poems are meant to be read by two people.
One person reads the lines in one color on the left,
alternating with the other person, who reads the lines in
another color on the right. The lines in the center of the
page, with letters in both colors, are read simultaneously.

Pansy and Poppy

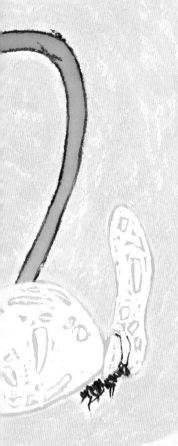

Straighten up, Poppy!
You're starting to flop.

> I'm feeling full, Pansy,
> as though I might pop.

I know what you mean.
My pods are a load.

> Oh, my! Do you think
> we're about to explode?

Don't worry, Poppy —
it won't hurt a bit.
When they're ready and ripe
our seed pods will split . . .

> and open like magic . . .
> *but then I'll be dead!*

Who put *that* foolishness into your head?
You'll be back next season!

> Will my seeds come back, too?

They'll grow into flowers.

> Yahoo!

We Can Fly

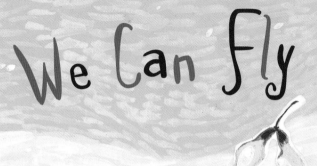

I fly by helicoptering.

   I move by parachute.

I took off from a maple tree
inside my whirling suit.

   I launched *my* gentle journey
   from a dandelion's head.

I rotate as I travel.

   I choose to drift instead.

Well, I've met gliders on *my* trips.

   And *I've* watched spinners spin.

No matter how seeds fly around . . .

We're carried by the wind.

Bye, Bye, Berries

I'm feeling tense.

Oh, just relax. Hang loose, now.
Please don't gripe.
Can't you see the sun and rain
have made us plump and ripe?

It's true! I'm looking perfect.

You have grown into a treat,
filled up with fruity little seeds
that birds can't wait to eat.

Oh, dear! I guess my end is near.

Yes. I'll be gone soon, too.
But our seeds will travel in the birds
and be dropped off in their doo.

Eeew!

Hitchhikers

I'm tired of hanging out here.

> Do you know a better place?
> Besides, we're stuck—we're cockleburs.

I'm not asking you to *race*!
I'm just saying we could travel.

> But we don't have feet or wings!

Then we'll have to hitch a ride
by grabbing on to moving things.

> Okay! I'll cling to this dog's fur.

I'll stick to those wool socks.

> Of all the ways seeds get around . . .

Our way really rocks!

Seedlings

Let's get out of these coats.

> I'm not ready. Please wait!

It's easy. I'll show you.
Watch me germinate.

> Wow! You're *amazing*.
> What's that hanging down?

Tiny roots that will keep me
attached to the ground.

> And now?

I'm unfurling!
My shoot's sprouting free.
Are *you* ready yet?

> Yes, definitely!

New Shoot

It's springtime!
Will you be up soon?
I feel sure you'll be cute.

> My roots are growing as we speak.
> I'm about to pop my shoot.
> Thanks for your concern, though.
> Will we meet when I come out?

Absolutely! Yessiree!
Of that I have no doubt.

> I can hardly wait to meet you.
> Yikes! I'm pushing through the earth.

Your little seed coat has come loose.
What an exciting birth!

> Ah! The air feels great! The sun is warm.
> It's beautiful up here!
> But back off now. You're crowding me.
> I don't want you this near.

Do you taste as tender as you look?

> Shoo! You're blocking my sunlight.

Relax. That doesn't matter.
You'll be gone in just one bite.

Daffodil Bulbs

It's dark here!

        You're right. That's true.

It's cold here!

        Not much to do.

It's dull here!

        Yes, things are slow.

It's cramped here!

        No room to grow.

        It's time now!

                Can you be sure?

        I know it!

                You're so mature.

        Good-bye now.

                I'm coming, too!

        Let's push now.

                We're breaking through!

It's bright here.

I see the sun.

It's warm here.

The winter's done!

It's spring here.

I feel so mellow.

We'll bloom here.

Wheeee! Let's be yellow.

Roots

I get no attention.

                You're hidden. It's true.

I'm gnarly and twisted.

                But all plants need you.

Plants take me for granted—
they don't give two hoots!

                Until gardeners move them
                and dig up their roots.
                They can't live without you!

That's true, very true.

                You store food for those plants!

I anchor them, too.
My looks aren't important.
I have other strengths.

                You're tough and can grow
                to incredible lengths.

I feel a lot better! Thanks mainly to you,
I'm proud to be doing what a root's meant to do.

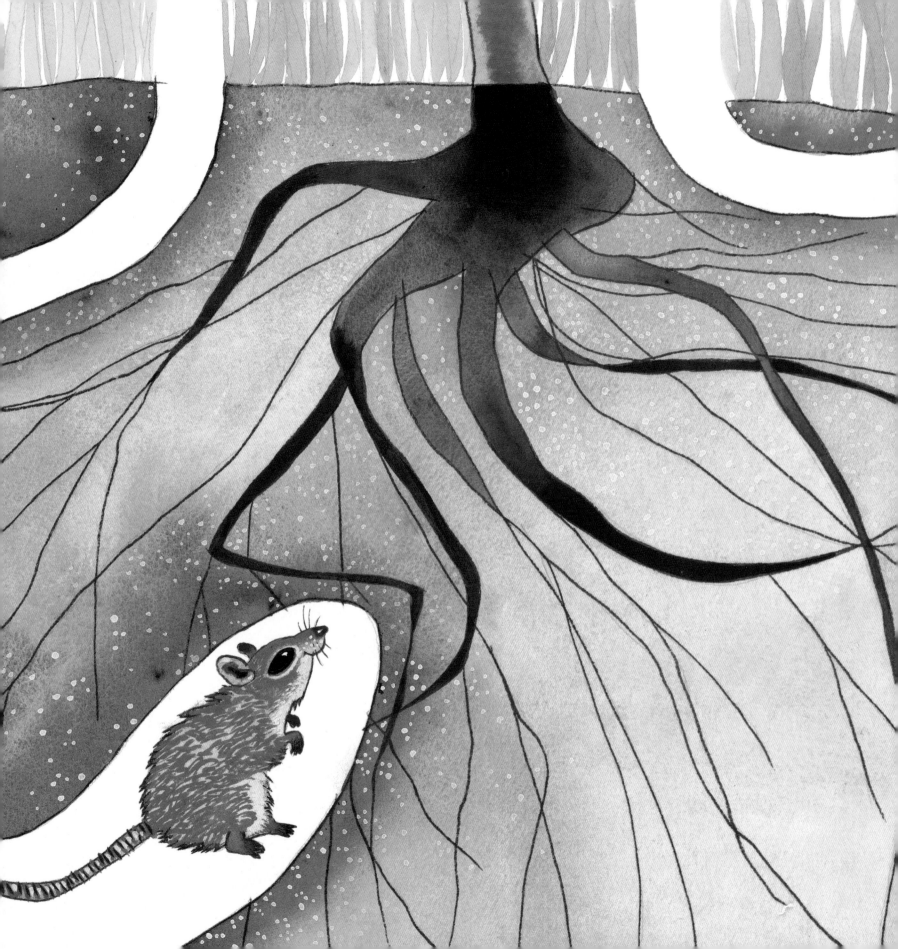

Helianthus

We get our start from small white seeds.

Then up we shoot! We grow like weeds.

At summer's end, we stand ten feet!

Our petals are yellow. Our faces are sweet.

In fall, we stoop. Our faces droop . . .

with seeds that feed all birds that need . . .

food. We're tasty!

People like us, too. Do you?

If saying "helianthus" makes you cower . . .

use our common name—

Sunflower!

Honey and Bumble

I like your black and yellow suit.

I love your tiny waist. Next to you,
I'm awkward and I take up too much space.

Bumble, you're a perfect bee.

Thanks, Honey, so are you.
Want to share my flower?
There's room enough for two!

Bee Balm

I'm drawn to your color.

Do you like my smell?

It's great!
Stupendous!
Totally swell!

You flatter me, Bee.

Every word's true.
Just ask the hummingbirds—
they love you, too!

Honeybee Dance

You're flying in a pattern.
Is that shape a figure eight?

Yes, it's a special bee dance
meant to communicate . . .

We get it now—directions!
You're showing where to go . . .

I'm sending you straight to the field
where clover flowers grow.

We'll gather all their nectar
and also pollinate,
with little tongues and little feet.

Want me to demonstrate?

No. We know how to do this work,
so we'll be on our way.
We're leaving for that field right now.

Have a busy, buzzy day!

Always Hungry

I am starving!

I am famished!

All we do is eat, eat, eat.

What we feed on is convenient.

It grows beneath our feet.

Its leaves and sap sustain us.

It's the only food we need.

It's our breakfast, lunch, and dinner.

It's the plant we love.

Milkweed!

Now We're Sleepy

I am drowsy.

I am sleepy.

Both of us have had our fill
of crawling, creeping, eating.

It's time now to be still.

I'm curling up beneath a leaf.

I'm snuggling down to nap.

No more crunching.

No more chewing.

No more drinking milkweed sap.

Hey! Are you asleep yet?

No, I'm in a sack! What's *this*?

It's what our skin turned into.

It's called a chrysalis.

I feel cozy in this thing.

Mine's exactly the right size.

Good night. Sweet dreams.

Sleep tight now.

Soon, we'll be butterflies!

New Baby

That's an odd-looking leaf
hanging from that old tree.

What could that strange thing possibly be?

It's wiggling. Waggling.
Looks ready to burst.

Let's hunker down low.
Prepare for the worst!

See! Something popped out.

I'm shaking with dread.
I hope we'll be safe in this flower bed.

Look now! It's gorgeous.

Eeek! It's flapping nearby!

It's coming to visit.

Hello, Butterfly!

Bedmates

Stop eating my compost!

It's my autumn snack.

It's my winter blanket, and I want it back!

Your bloom time is over. You look nearly dead.

I'll be back next summer—get out of my bed!

I'll have to come first to plow up the ground.
Without my help, Flower, you'd not be around.

Okay! You can stay, Worm.
But where will you go
when wintertime comes and it starts to snow?

I'll rest, just as you do. I'll tunnel down deep,
curl up near your roots, and have a long sleep.

In the meantime, dear Worm, I'll kindly feed you.
More compost?

Thanks, Flower. Don't mind if I do!

Who's There?

Something's on my bottom leaf.

Something's crawling up *my* stem!

Could it be those nasty bugs?
I thought we'd gotten rid of them.

I don't feel wings.

I don't feel feet.

They're moving kind of slow.

Just then, I felt a bit of slime . . .

Me, too! Oh, no! Oh, no!

You know that stuff we felt just now?

Those icky, sticky trails?

They're not put down by bugs or worms.
They're left behind by . . .

SNAILS!

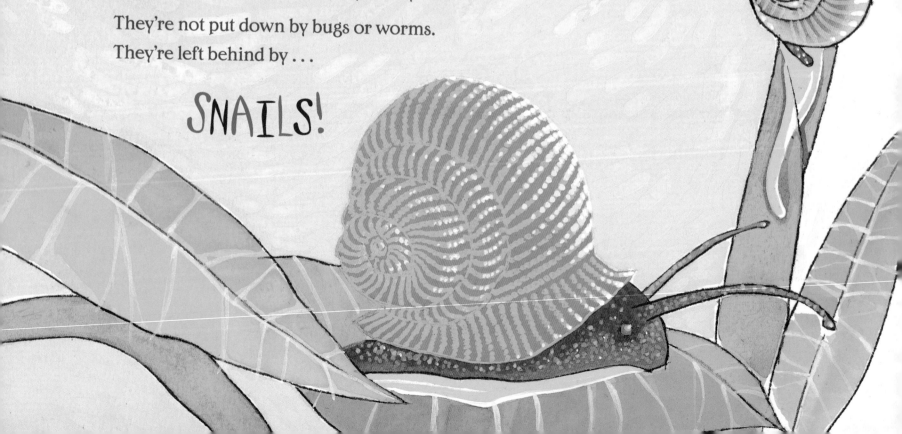

Ladybug Hugs

If garden flowers could give hugs . . .

we'd embrace the ladybugs.

Every summer, without fuss,
they eat the pests that chew on us.

They look harmless. They look sweet.

But all those ladies do is eat!

Each chomps aphids—five per hour!

An amazing number to devour.

When summer's over, off they'll go.

We'll miss those hungry ladies so!

M ost plants—from the biggest trees to the smallest flowers—produce seeds. Some seeds are tiny. Others are large. Inside each is the beginning of a baby plant.

Seeds travel in different ways. Some are bought or gathered by people and planted in fields or gardens. Others drop off and grow beside their parent plants. Many seeds are carried by wind, water, or animals to grow in other places.

A coat covers each seed. Seed coats protect and nourish the tiny plants inside. When the time is right, little shoots and small roots break through the seed coats.

The roots soak up minerals and water from the soil. The slender shoots reach toward the sun. In time, if conditions are right, leaves and flowers grow on the plant. Many flowers produce fruit to hold their seeds.

The female parts of most flowers produce sweet nectar. Nectar attracts bees, butterflies, and other critters. The male parts of flowers produce a sticky powder called pollen.

Pollen sticks to the feet and bodies of bees and other creatures that gather or eat the nectar. As the creatures move from flower to flower, pollen drops onto the female parts and fertilizes them. In this way, flowering parts of plants bear seeds. From these seeds, new plants will grow. Nature repeats this process year after year.